T0067174

Poetic Justice

Lessons of love, life & relationships

Poetic Justice

Lessons of love, life & relationships

Tami Belt

BALBOA.
PRESS

A DIVISION OF HAY HOUSE

Balboa Press books may be ordered through booksellers or by contacting:

Balboa Press
A Division of Hay House
1663 Liberty Drive
Bloomington, IN 47403
www.balboapress.com
1 (877) 407-4847

Because of the dynamic nature of the Internet, any web addresses or links contained in this book may have changed since publication and may no longer be valid. The views expressed in this work are solely those of the author and do not necessarily reflect the views of the publisher, and the publisher hereby disclaims any responsibility for them.

The author of this book does not dispense medical advice or prescribe the use of any technique as a form of treatment for physical, emotional, or medical problems without the advice of a physician, either directly or indirectly. The intent of the author is only to offer information of a general nature to help you in your quest for emotional and spiritual well-being. In the event you use any of the information in this book for yourself, which is your constitutional right, the author and the publisher assume no responsibility for your actions.

Print information available on the last page.

ISBN: 978-1-5043-2708-4 (sc)
ISBN: 978-1-5043-2709-1 (e)

Library of Congress Control Number: 2015905702

Balboa Press rev. date: 11/10/2015

Loyalty begins with an authentic story.
Tami Belt revisits her storytelling roots in Poetic Justice
by sharing her journey in hopes of inspiring everyone
to find their authentic voice.
— Jackie Huba, author of *Monster Loyalty: How Lady Gaga
Turns Followers into Fanatics*

Just a moment. That's all it will take to be swept up
by the grace and simple elegance of Poetic Justice.
Tami Belt has heard the music of our lives
and returns it to us wrapped in love.
— Bill Jensen, author of *Simplicity and The Courage Within Us*

A poem is just a poem, unless it conveys
its deepest feelings from author to reader -
like a song that brings back familiar memories.
Tami Belt has composed a heart-felt song through Poetic Justice.
— Eric Dahl, author of *B.B. King's Lucille and the Loves Before Her*

With her new book, Las Vegas writer Tami Belt showcases her
sensitivity and creativity. She brings real emotion and color to every
page.
— John L. Smith
Las Vegas Review-Journal columnist and author of *Vegas Voices:
Conversations with Great Las Vegas Characters*

Dedication

This book is dedicated to my Grandparents for providing the spaces where my childhood imagination could run wild - from backyard bamboo jungles and the bee place to the basement bomb shelter and dining room forts to the cabin in the mountains by a creek.

To Julie and Betty for your unconditional friendship, believing in me until I believed in myself and for all the Rainbows sent from Heaven.

Special thanks to Nina and her mad organizing skills over an epic weekend that kept the pages of this book turning.

Much gratitude and love to Jennifer Main for artistically translating my intention for this book into an extraordinary work of art. You can view her work at www.jennifermaingallery.com.

Contents

I did not write these poems, they wrote me.

Chapter 1

A Way With Words

I think I'm going
to write a poem
to tell the world
I'm all alone

Then maybe if
my poem gets read
I can make someone care
and bow their head

And if I'm lucky
they'll come to me
and take my hand
and set me free

And then we'd walk
and laugh and live
and I would have someone
to take what I give

Then I could sit
and write another poem
so everyone in the world
wouldn't have to be alone

When nobody listened I told the Universe.

I wish I could
sing you a song
but to say all the words
would take too long

I wish I could
paint you a scene
but colors can't explain
exactly what I mean

I wish I could
write you a poem
and read it to you
when we're all alone

But words
you cannot feel
the same way as me
for to me they're real

I wish I could
just give you a touch
to show you
what I want so much

I wish I could
have you enter my dreams
and dream with me
all that it seems

Then you could
know how I feel
and maybe to you
I would seem real

But tomorrow
I'll only ask again
and you will be there
just my friend

Healing Words

I wish I could kiss your cheek
and wash away your tears
hold you close within my arms
and gently rock away your fears

If you hold me in your thoughts
I'll help to ease your mind
sending waves of comfort
inner warmth you will find

Imagine your soft lips to mine
and feel a rush of joy
as burdens melt away
embrace the freedom of a boy

Mere written words
are emotions you cannot feel
with the same intensity as me
for to me they're far more real

So I'll send you a song
created in my heart
whenever you feel lonely
you'll know we're not far apart

Imagination colors our stories.

Imagine

I can imagine
things so wild
like the uninhibited mind
of an untouched child

Before their spirit is broken
by an adult's reality
their imagination can soar
just like the one in me

This cold world has broken
many happy minds
and placed them in a world
controlled by its times

A monetary existence
of selfish acts
where once you are captured
you can never go back

But I've escaped
I set myself free
I can show you
what no others can see

For beyond the time clocks
and the monetary flow
is an imaginary world
that only children know

So before you teach them
of your knowledge so vast
take a look
way back deep into your past

Just once more
let your imagination run wild
before you teach
all you know to your child

I want to write a poem
to tell you how I feel
because to me
these feelings are real

I want to tell of the love
I want to tell of the hate
of being lonely
and not wanting to wait

I want to tell
of getting older
signs on my face
and my heart growing colder

I want to tell
of bitter revenge
I want to go back
to a long-ago friend

This isn't working
writing makes me hurt
I don't want the pain back
my thoughts I must divert

All those days
and all those nights
my writing filled me
with sorrow and fright

That's when I lost touch
and lost my feel
I lived in a dream
where nothing was real

I pretended my poems
took away my tears
but every night
I thought of new fears

The more I wrote
the harder I cried
and with each new poem
a part of me died

I was trying to tell you
to stop hurting me
but your eyes were different
you just couldn't see

Now it's started again
the pain, I mean
maybe you've grown enough
to understand what I've seen

Poets Are Madmen

Poets are madmen
who see visions and dreams
they look inside of souls
and tell you what it means

A psychotic little world
no one can understand
they bring the strong to their knees
it's a universal plan

Tears of joy and sorrow
aren't expressions of grief
as they make the masses wonder
and stare in disbelief

You think you understand
the translation of their words
but if you read between the lines
you might see what they want heard

In desperation they try
merely to fit in
a normal reality
to a poet is a sin

For without the experience
of places where most run and hide
the poet can never express
your deepest feelings inside

Thoughts of lust and freedom
tears of grief and joy
the hidden soul comes to life
you lost with your childhood toys

Dare to taste their wine
and drink from their cup
at a table set for one
you'll never grow up

If you don't own your feelings
they will consume you.
They will take root in your
soul and imprison you.

Chapter 2

Friendship

A Special Kind of Friend

There's a special kind of friendship
in which words you need not share
where a special bond of love is made
to show how much you care

Throughout this friendship with bonded love
even if harsh words are spoken
the special friendship is always there
for the bond cannot be broken

Why do we need words anyhow
to show how much you care
If you know the feeling and it's strong
what else do you need to show it's there

So later on, after many years
even after we've both gone
every time you think of me
you'll find the bond still strong

For like true love, a special friendship
can never be replaced
the feelings and memories are forever with you
no matter the time and space

Collect memories, people can fade. Memories take root in your heart and grow fonder with each season of your life.

Come to Me

I'll always be here
for you
to talk to

I'll always listen
to what you have
to say
and I'll try to
help you in every way

But you have
to come to me
and trust me

I can't come
to you

But once you make
that step to me
I promise
I'll never
let you down

I'll never
forget you
I can't forget you

That would be
like forgetting
my growing up

Yes we've been
through a lot
and I know
it hasn't all been good
but it hasn't all been bad

But it's after
the bad
that we appreciate
things we have more

So don't ever forget
about me
and if there's ever anything
no matter how small
please don't hesitate to
call me

I need somebody
coming to me
as much as you need
someone to go to

It all started
when I used to call you on the phone
because it was night
and I was scared to be alone

I was confused then
the world was going too fast
so you slowed it down
by saying our friendship would last

For that meant
that I could come to you
and you'd help out by telling me
things I never knew

And from those things
our friendship grew
a long lasting one
with a love I thought true

I can't afford gifts
all shiny and new
so I will share
my gift with you

My gift came
from up above
and it is filled
with the perfect love

This love I feel
inside my heart
will be felt by you
before I depart

Please treasure my gift
as I have done
and everyone will learn
of your special one

I hope my gift
can make you smile
and stop the worry
for just a little while

This isn't packaged with curly bows
or wrapped in red and blue
it's just a little part of me
I wanted to share with you

People don't know what's best for you. You know what's best for you. Let your knowledge blossom.

You touched me
deep inside my heart
your tender loving kindness
in me remains a part

You loved me
when I didn't love myself
you opened my eyes to life
and took me off a shelf

You showed me
what no one else could see
that I had something special
hidden deep inside of me

You listened
when I thought no one could hear
my cries for love and acceptance
you wiped away my fear

You left this world
without a regret
Our friendship transcends time
I'll never forget

Like Sisters

She hasn't always
been there
She's sometimes left me
to be by myself

Other times
she'll share the pain
other times
she'll create it

But no matter what
she really cares
she really understands
because she was once there

She too, had to go through
the pain
and she too
had to hurt people along the way

People she loved
and people I loved
sometimes I hated her for it
sometimes I didn't understand

She's always tried
to help me
if she thinks
she really can

Or she'll tell me
to help myself
that's when
I start to feel bad

When I see
how much I asked of her
and how much she gave me
when I realized it too late

I was always too concerned
with myself, my own pain
and hated her sometimes
for the things she told me

Even though I knew
that she was right
I didn't want
to hear it

Because it
hurt me
but I never realized until later
that it hurt her, too

Sometimes it hurt her
more than me
because that's how much
she cares about me

Just like sisters
at times
we loved
and hated each other

Sentimental Moments

Sentimental moments
and good time spent with you
make tomorrow brighter
because of all you helped me through

Sentimental moments
and teardrops we have shed
renew a lasting friendship
to the present which we are led

Sentimental moments
we treasure in our hearts
can only be reassuring
knowing they can't be torn apart

Sentimental moments
from the past will always be
of a special friendship
that was shared between you and me

The Good-Bye People

In each precious lifetime
there are only a few
special people, I mean
just like you

Those you can count on
to brighten your day
their memories are enough
to light your way

Their stay is always too brief
but their impact so strong
they will never be forgotten
in your heart they belong

These good-bye people
are always around
to give you strength
when you start to feel down

To know this kind of friendship
is a special bond
which can never be broken
no matter how long they're gone

These good-bye people
always mean the most
they can never go away
after a meaningless toast

Out of sight
but never out of mind
you will always be
this special kind

Just thank God
they stayed for a while
and thank them for letting you
make them smile

Don't feel sad
when they move on
it's their turn to shine
in tomorrow's new dawn

As the sun rises
their journey begins again
to brighten more lives
their job never ends

I'm glad I had the chance
to encounter your smile
and be your friend
for just a little while

You always enrich
the lives of those you touch
may you never forget
those who love you so much

There's no time for tears
as we reminisce
on the special moments
you have made the best

May rainbows flourish in your future
and freebirds abound
all you have to do is remember
and loved ones will be around

The childhood dreams
you treasured yesterday
now seem so distant
and so far away

You want to move ahead
but you want to hold on
with all the pain and confusion
you wonder how you'll get along

But that's why I'm here
to help you decide
what to do next
in me you can confide

You're growing up gradually
like everyone does
trying to be different from yesterday
when you don't always know what it was

Yesterday you tried
to get the boy
but it never hurt
when you lost that toy

But that was before
and the boy can't stand
he falls down too much
so for tomorrow you want a man

You say you can handle it
but it's not the same
the game never changes
it just increases in pain

Now the stakes are higher
there's quite a rise in price
for to play this game
it's yourself you must sacrifice

So don't try looking
for something you're not ready to find
think carefully about my advice
and keep it in mind

I know you're grown up
so don't try and prove it
you have so much going for you
I don't want you to lose it

Chapter 3

Longing

I want to be
awaken by a kiss
I want to hear
that it's me you miss

I want someone
to hold me close
and make me feel
I mean the most

I need the confidence
of an encouraging word
not of needed improvements
of those, I've already heard

I need to share
the joys of someone's life
not be burdened with
someone's struggle and strife

I never had a chance to share
in someone else's dreams
only in their struggle
filled with fights and screams

I want someone who is
through with their climb
and has the opportunity
to share with me their time

It's my turn to be helped
like I've done for so many before
I want to be taken care of
as I try to find my door

I want the same chances
that I have given them
I need someone to be
just as good of a friend

I want it to be their sacrifice
when we go out at night
not always mine
when I turn out the light

I want no more pain
I want no more to give
I just want to take
and finally begin to live

Heartbreaks will heal.
Betrayals take longer.

For Your Smile

For your smile
I'd stop time
freeze-frame each moment
to see your light shine

For your touch
each day I long
cherishing every encounter
in your arms I want to belong

For your kiss
sweet anticipation
a heartfelt connection
now I'm afraid to mention

For your time
the greatest gift to share
wondering who
you're longing could be there

For your love
someone waits for the day
for your heart to know
the words they long you'll say

Come Closer

Come closer to me
grab my hand and help me through
lead me closer
to be ready for you

Help me grow
and realize what it means
to finally be ready
to reach my dreams

Why is it my journey
to undertake alone
please meet me halfway
I've already grown

I don't want to travel alone
to meet you at the end
why can't you guide me
so we can begin

I'm ready despite
what others say
I believe in my heart
I'm ready today

Help heal my heart
together it can mend
no longer do I wish
to wait and pretend

I was in love once
and it was great
but something happened
and it changed to hate

At first it hurt
I couldn't bear the pain
but now I don't care
why I can't explain

It still feels good
to be held in your arms
but I can't let myself
fall victim to your charms

Wedding bells and friendship rings
are again a decision to make
but this time I'll be careful
my heart can't stand another break

I loved you once
and it was fun
but this fight is more serious
I have to know I've won

I know that love is present
inside both of our hearts
but is it strong enough
to make a new start

Absence makes
the heart grow colder
with each and every
turn of a shoulder

That same shoulder
that used to hold my head
and lie bare next to me
as I slept in your bed

Whatever happened
to the loving arms
that were always waiting
to protect me from harms

Those soft lips
that wanted to touch mine
just slipped away
to a long-ago time

Absence from these things
and many more
make it difficult
to open another door

Suddenly you stopped
wanting me around
that's when I began
to need to be found

You wanted to with others
things you wouldn't with me
and you couldn't understand
how it can hurt so deeply

Sometimes it seems
that love is just a game
where there are no rules
but we loose just the same

There is no game so bitter
than one driven by desire
letting go can't be done
because heart's feelings never tire

Understanding, not pity
I wanted you to see
just to hold me a little longer
is all I wanted for me

Closer to the Heart

From the breakup we had
we need a new start
I need to become
closer to the heart

Closer to the heart
of the one I've always loved
to that special person
sent to me from above

Closer to the heart
and nearer to the soul
of the only person
who has the power to make me whole

Love may hurt
but in the end
you always seem
to make me smile again

So after forever
to make it last
we'll build a stairway to heaven
and learn from our past

Sometimes there's days
when I long for a touch
not often, mind you
when I want so much

Bad day on earth school
if you know what this means
Then come and comfort me
alone in my screams

Tears are too painful
to express anymore
I keep them locked behind
a protected prison door

The pain behind the words
I can no longer bear
a life long ago left
I'm still crying there

Take away my fears
listen to my words
I don't want to be rescued
I just want to be heard

If someone can understand
then I won't feel alone
no longer cast aside
I just want to come home

All my dreams
have come to pass
none stayed long
enough to last

I tried like hell
to make them come true
but nobody would let them
not even you

Nobody needed my help
or the love I gave
it might be too late now
is there enough to save

The pieces were shattered
and just thrown about
pieces of dreams and a love
I couldn't live without

Nobody needed
or wanted to love me
they just walked away
and let me be

So out of this world
I exit without fear
if you want to think of me
I'll always be near

But to only those few
who I really love
will I be near to
and watch over from above

No tears, no pity
no sorrow, no grief
will be present
after I leave

But that's alright
I already knew that
that's why I'm leaving
and not coming back

Out of your life
I've now come to be
I won't be famous, hated, loved
or remembered in anyone's history

Touch Me

Mere words could never translate
the emotions evoked by touch
the absence of a longing for
what I need so much

The basic primal need
of human satisfaction
takes so may forms
results in so many reactions

Diversion or acceptance
the answer we'll never know
until the risk is taken
your spirit will die or grow

Music looks inside your soul
and opens up your heart
it eliminates all distance
if you can feel a part

A touch transcends time
wounds it can heal
to your knees you'll fall
if you can touch something real

Expression is a catharsis for your soul.

There were so many things
that I wished I'd said
when we were together
alone in bed

I knew this would happen
it always does
people come and go
and I remember what was

Just a few days ago
you were within my touch
but now you're out of reach
and I want you so much

I'm tired of being used
and getting left behind
people leave my sight
but they're never out of mind

All it would take
is a call on the phone
to stop this feeling
of being hopelessly alone

You made me feel
like nobody else before
you finally shed some light
through a long closed door

I really thought you cared
I never felt a doubt
but now I'm wondering
what it was all about

Was there someone waiting
for you to return home
is that why it's my turn
to sit here all alone

I don't believe you're like that
you seem more than a friend
I just can't stand wondering
and trying to pretend

Love doesn't hurt, lies do.

Out of the Blue

Out of the blue
and into the light
coming into focus
what was once out of sight

Out of sight
but always in mind
you appeared out of nowhere
with words so kind

A smile so sweet
it pierces the walls
constructed long ago
from too many falls

How do I begin
to translate my expression
of the innermost feelings
my heart dares not mention

You live in the moment
but before I can start
I need to know
what is my part

Letting myself feel
your body touching mine
a desire for your caress
creates the rhythm of my rhyme

The ecstasy of your touch
soft lips against my skin
afraid you'll leave
as soon as I let you in

Please catch me if I fall
outside my comfort zone
for you've led me to a place
where it's not safe for me alone

It's easy for me to fall
when I feel what's inside
despite the fear I'm trying
to just enjoy the ride

Too afraid to write
what I don't yet know
wanting to hold on
scared of letting go

For when I open up
it's heart, mind and soul
each time I die
each time I grow

Feelings now scare me
I know the power of their pain
just when I lost touch
I'm not able to explain

The contradiction of connection
I can't find the right word
I'm not asking for forever
Just to be heard

Putting my feelings
out in the universe
is the purpose of my prose
for better or for worse

I'll take your hand to lead me
for this moment in time
on an unknown journey
for today, please be mine

*Why do I always
have to hold on tight
It only makes me lonely
as I lie awake at night*

*When can I let go
of my little childhood dreams
and finally realize
nothing is what it seems*

*I wish I could explain
to those who aren't around
that I always want them near
and I want to be found*

*But rainbows blind my eyes
and forever is too far away
I'm afraid of the answers
so I'll be alone again today*

*Will anyone I find
ever share my dream
who can understand
exactly what I mean*

Rainbows are forever
and as far as I can see
they will last in heaven
and be colored by you and me

Sometimes I'm too selfish
and I expect too much
I can't leave well enough alone
after I feel the first little touch

I keep holding on
to tomorrow's dreams
and I want forever
to be more than what it seems

Treat me with kindness
respect and love
shower me with happiness
from the heavens above

For I am the Golden Bird
I am the Dove
I live only
to be worthy of your love

Freedom and Love
are all I need to survive
as long as you provide them
I know I'll stay alive

I've treated you special
but now the tables are turned
it's my turn to be treated special
with the love that I've earned

So treat me gentle
and show me that you care
never let me forget
that you'll always be there

I know I'm special
but I'm not trying to boast
I'm just trying to hold on
to the love I need the most

Paint. Dance. Sing. Write. Do whatever you have to do to set your story free.

Alone I Dream

Alone I wake
and face the dawn
remembering a dream
that is long gone

Alone I walk
out of the door
forgetting a dream
that doesn't matter anymore

Alone I enter
the outside world
waiting for a new dream
to be unfurled

Alone I return
to my faded dreams
where life is old
and not what it seems

Alone I sleep
all through the night
dreaming that tomorrow
won't be filled with fright

Alone I dream
my life away
please somebody come
and make my dream stay

Alone in the night
my dream slowly dies
each night alone
with tears in my eyes

Alone in the day
my dream becomes a blur
everyday it seems unlikely
that a new dream will occur

Alone in my tomorrow
is my dream for today
please no one come
and take my dream away

Chapter 4

Listen to Me

I Have a Dream

I have a dream
and that dream is life
to get the most
is for what I strive

I have a dream
and it is to live
I'm starting to take
and let someone else give

I have a dream
and it is to grow
I will reach the top
before I let go

I have a dream
and it is to laugh
no more will I walk
alone on my path

I have a dream
and it is hope
never again will I feel
I'm at the end of my rope

I have a dream
and it is for you
whatever you dream
I hope will come true

I have learned that it's not what happens to you but what you think happened. Everything is a matter of perspective.

63

I hate it when you do
the little things you do
because my true feelings
always show through

Love is not something
to be punished for
If you take it for granted
it will be no more

It's hard to cope
and stay around
when the one you love
can't settle down

After I leave
will you regret
the way you acted
those nights we met

Will you ever think
that you were wrong
or will you forget me
as soon as I'm gone

I don't want to rush you
but my patience is low
so help me through
or I might have to go

I know you need time
to figure things out
but when you don't call
I have my doubts

If you don't listen to yourself, who will?
Pay attention to all the thoughts that drift through your head.
They appear for a reason.

Let me get away
and for once be by myself
I'm tired of hiding
the real me on a shelf

I want to love
I want to learn
Everyone has to grow up
now it's my turn

Let me go
no questions asked
The best thing for me
is to forget my past

It's driving me crazy
how can't you see
you're turning me into something
I don't want to be

I know I'm not a baby
when I cry myself to sleep
I just get tired of fighting off
the hold on me you keep

I need some fresh air
I want to make a start
I want to live the life
I know is right in my heart

I need you as a friend
I need you as a brother
I need you for security
I need you as a lover

I need you
to help me along
I need your touch
and to hear our song

I need to laugh
I need to sing
I need someone
to take the love I bring

I want you by me
I need your love
I want you back
so we can live above

I need your arm around me
I want to be your strength again
I want to start over
and be more than a friend

I'm tired of being lonely
I don't want to play a game
I need us to change
so things won't turn out the same

The time has come
for this love to end
it's time for us to start
to begin again

Together or alone
we both must carry on
but we have to do something
before everything is gone

We shared a great friendship
we shared a great love
but there was always something missing
a blessing from above

I hate to let go
but sometimes I feel I must
I feel that that's the only way
I can get back your faith and trust

Too much hate was created
too much love was destroyed
nothing makes us happy now
before it was only each other we enjoyed

I'm not trying to be cold
I don't want to hurt you
I'm not even saying
that our love's completely through

I'm just trying to find out
what is best for me
whether it's being all alone
or loving you for eternity

Chapter 5

Rhythm & Rhyme

The Music Man

Inspiration breeds
blood, sweat and tears
if you listen to the music
you can do much more than hear

A journey through time
a joyous, painful past
makes the future seem so bright
in each note the feeling lasts

Let the music man play
and experience the tune
lay back on a blanket
and gaze into the moon

Think beyond your feelings
and look into his eyes
listen to the notes he plays
and try to realize

Inspiration breeds
blood sweat and tears
if you listen to the music
you can do much more than hear

Each note has a story
a bitter-sweet end
a new beginning
then it starts over again

Hey music man tell me
what you think it means
as you play your life away
was it all that you had dreamed

Play your hopes and dreams for me
and I will try to feel
the emotion of your music
that makes your life so real

Beyond the smoke and crowded rooms
beyond the sweat and pain
your music touches hearts
a mere memory will remain

A universal gift
inside each and every note
your music fills their souls
to each song your life devote

Is it worth it music man
to relive your life in song
do you feel lonely
or are you where you belong

Inspiration breeds
blood, sweat and tears
if you listen to the music
you can do much more than hear

Do you see an end
or is tomorrow just the same
every day expose your life
music . . . by just another name

Tell me how you feel
your inspiration and desire
what compels you every day
to burn with such a fire

Inspiration breeds
blood, sweat and tears
if you listen to the music
you can do much more than hear

Do you want someone to see
someone to understand
the loneliness and joy
someone to hold your hand

Play me a dream
as I lay down to sleep
the notes will linger on
in my memory they will keep

Inspiration breeds
blood, sweat and tears
if you listen to the music
you can do much more than hear

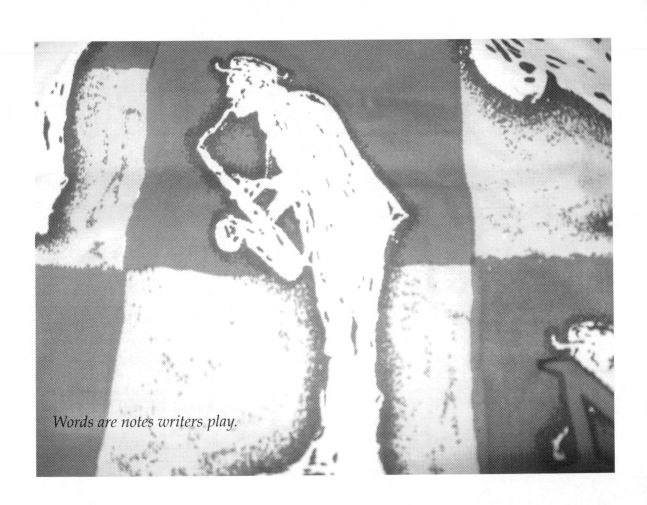

Words are notes writers play.

You blew me away
one night in June
wine and warm summer breezes
and a saxophone tune

Phone calls everyday
heighten anticipation
of a caring touch
feelings I dare not mention

An afternoon in the mountains
a night in Tahoe
I'll never understand
how I couldn't know

Promises of Paris
days of sipping wine
listening to you play
knowing you're not mine

Thanks for the memories
and making me feel
that I really mattered
in your life I was real

Never before
and maybe never again
I felt I could be more
than just a friend

Listen to My Music

Listen to my music
and hear what it can do
Let them make their own music
and do what's right for you

Listen to my music
and feel my power grow
Let it teach you, keep it with you
never let it go

Listen to my music
remember all the words
friendly faces, special places
the words you've always heard

Listen to my music
and share my life with me
think about me, keep me with you
but just in memory

Listen to my music
for it tells of the past
falling teardrops, special rainbows
times we can't win back

Listen to my music
for no more will it be heard
live your life so I won't have to
again say love's a word

Listen to my music
just one final time
for you won't miss me, you don't have to
say that you'll be mine

There's a rhythm to every rhyme.

Sweet Saxations

Each touch of the cold steel
I feel against my flesh
you feel the ecstasy of the audience
I feel our bodies mesh

Your connection is different
unconditional satisfaction
the applause is your fulfillment
mine a one-on-one connection

Let me be your audience
your solo focus of attention
Play me what you feel
what words could never mention

Is it uncertainty
is it joy or fire
is anyone enough
to satisfy your desire

You touch me with your music
as you do with your skin
I want you to feel me
when you play from within

Melancholy tunes
are left in my heart
each time I see you
means more time apart

One way or another your story will emerge.
Your song cannot be silenced.

CLOSURE

You started a song
many years ago
was it fast and filled with life
or was it sad and slow

As days pass by
I don't remember
the last time I touched you
was it August or September?

Please define me
a musical expression
how would you translate
what words could never mention

A musical interpretation
of feelings inside
the notes are the walls
behind which you hide

I want to understand
your feelings from within
the hidden soul
where feelings begin

Please write the notes
finish the song
without closure
I'm lost and don't belong

Chapter 6

Rainbows

I color the rainbows
after the storm
and give them away
with a smile so warm

I push aside the clouds
and let the colors show through
please let me give
a rainbow to you

I want you to learn
of their secret light
that always keeps you smiling
when you're lonely at night

Please build me a rainbow
to brighten my day
then when I'm alone
I'll know you're not far away

To build a rainbow
you only need to care
and you only need to want
to always be there

I have given many rainbows
but up until today
everyone has kept
my rainbows far away

No one has returned
the special gift of love
that would make me smile
when I look up above

Please build me a rainbow
so that I will know
that you want to be near me
and never let me go

I hope it's not too much
to ask for your smile
to be alone with me
for just a little while

Savor every sip of color in your life.
Fill your palette with surprise.

If rainbows are forever
and dreams are supposed to come true
then why can't I have one
made for me and you

So that after the raindrops
a smile will fill your face
and then I will feel
that I belong in one place

I'm tired of chasing rainbows
that have no pot of gold
will I ever find one
before I grow too old

I wish someone could see
the rainbow of my dreams
then you would realize
it's more special than it seems

Give Me Forever

We dreamers
have our ways
of facing
rainy days

But somehow I'll survive

I've turned the rain
into the sun
and created a rainbow
built for one

No one understands
its secret light
that keeps me shining
all through the night

If you hold my hand
all alone in the dark
I'll let you see
a tiny spark

For only I
hold the key
to the rainbow's world
beyond reality

I want to share
the secret light
but it takes more
than a couple of nights

It takes a lifetime
of togetherness
that can be started
by a special kiss

Please take my hand
when I'm alone at night
and I will share
my rainbow's light

Don't ever leave
from my side
for then me and my rainbow
will again have to hide

Please build me a rainbow
in the dark of night
and never let me go
as we gaze into the light

Let my rainbow blind you
just one day at a time
then slowly you will rise
with my freebird you will climb

I can take you places
that you've never seen
in my special little world
built only on a dream

All you have to do
is grab hold of my hand
and the journey will begin
to my distant land

It's a very special place
that no one else can see
I created in a dream
for only you and me

Tears wash away our pain
so our light can blossom.

I wished upon a rainbow
a long time ago
but my wish got lost
just where I don't know

I looked for years
for my dream to come true
maybe it will
with some help from you

If you help rebuild my rainbow
with all its colors so bright
and hold me close
through the darkness of night

If you hold my hand
when I'm scared in the dark
then maybe my dream
will begin to spark

And from that spark
will be a rekindled glow
remnants of the dream
I lost long ago

Please color my rainbow
with loving care
and keep the fire burning
by always being there

If we can bring my rainbow
back from its hiding place
I promise you a smile
will be felt upon your face

Then together we can share
the magic of my dream
and maybe you can feel
exactly what I mean

Rainbows Are Forever

Friendships that we make
time just takes away
but the Rainbows never leave
they were made to stay

Friendship pledges that we make
are only broken in the end
but the Rainbow shall return
to brighten your day again

I don't like broken promises
they only make me cry
so to you I only promise
what brightens up the sky

For in its modest glow
lies the power from above
of everlasting friendship
and that special kind of love

So I promise you a Rainbow
for all your rainy days
then you will remember me
when at its magic you stop to gaze

Rainbows bend over backwards to color
our dreams with possibility.

Color My Rainbow

On that distant day
when I must go
to help you remember me
I'll build you a rainbow

A special rainbow
with no colors in sight
the colors will only be visible
in true love's shining light

The rainbow will always
cover the sky above
waiting for you to color it
with the beautiful colors of love

You can color my rainbow
for everyone to see
all the beautiful colors of love
that was shared between you and me

I'll build you a rainbow
way up in the clouds
then you'll know I'm watching over you
and my love's all around

Chapter 7

Wishful Thinking

I Want Starry Nights

I want starry nights
and moonlight dances
holding hands
and romantic glances

I want caring arms
waiting to unfold
and special feelings
wanting to be told

I want picnic baskets
filled with cheese and wine
shared in a world
where there exists no time

I want parks at night
to swing on swings
and all the romance
that a moonlight walk brings

I want endless nights
dawned with laughter
two bodies entangled
in the morning after

I want weekends spent
in hide-a-way places
where dreams come true
to two smiling faces

I want all my dreams
to finally come true
I want them to be
set free by you

I wrote this poem for someone
I haven't met.
Sometimes you have to
color your own story.

Come take my hand
and escape with me
as I embark
on a never-ending journey

We'll enter a world
that has never been seen
except by me
alone in a dream

there we'll need nothing more
but each others' hand
as together we explore
my secret wonderland

Maybe we'll discover
the rainbow's magic light
and capture the glow
to shine for us in the night

The Free Bird will
let us ride on its wings
and we'll soar to secret places
and see magnificent things

Together we can share
each other's fantasy
in a special dream world
created by me

Uninhibited by time
or human concern
we can just be ourselves
and let the fire burn

We can surpass the limits
of the ordinary world
as we watch in amazement
our dreams being unfurled

We can escape forever
never to be returned
to the worrisome world
where only hell is learned

Alone we'll color
our own rainbow
a special gift
that no one else can know

So come fly with me
to my distant land
all you need to do
is grab hold of my hand

I grew up once. I didn't like it. I'll never do it again.

Wanted:

A friend to go out with
just for fun
someone to call when I'm lonely
that I know will always come

Someone to let me live
the childhood I never had
a friend to share good times with
someone who won't show me bad

Someone that can understand
all of life's ups and downs
a friend who will always be ready
to pick me up off the ground

I need someone to help me win
this game of life we play
I need someone to start tomorrow
I'm getting married today

What I hold on to
is the memory of a love
the you of yesterday
that only exists above

I know it's not right
to live inside the past
So I'll just keep the memory
because together we didn't last

I'm not saying to go back
to somewhere you don't belong
Just remember it's never too late
there's still time to change the road you're on

So listen to my music
each and every day
listen closely and let me help
guide you on your way

For I loved a different you
one that lies hidden inside
It might grow up or continue to be covered
up by some silly pride

So if you feel something
let it show
for if you keep it inside too long
I will have to go

Now I don't feel lonely
for I'll never lose my past
All I have to do is remember
and I might be loved back

Intuition has your best interest at heart.
Trust yourself. You know more than you think.

If you could wish
upon a star
and release your dreams
to the heavens afar

What would you hope
could come true
what dreams would you wish
just for you

What is your desire
to the universe declare
that's all you need to do
to manifest what you want there

Chapter 8

Questions

Why

Don't ask why
to someone close
for those are the ones
who hurt you the most

Don't ask when
you started to drift
there's too many feelings
through which you have to sift

Don't ask about the past
it happened long ago
there's been too many secrets
you might not want to know

Don't ask about attitudes
formed in the past
old habits die hard
tomorrow they will last

Don't ask about tomorrow
for it never comes
after too many questions
you're the lonely ones

I learned at a very young age that you can't help someone who won't help themselves. Sometimes the life you have to save is your own.

After we make love
you just walk away
you turn your back on me
and finish your day

No thoughts of me
are in your mind
to everyone, save yourself
you become totally blind

You go through your day
without a second thought
about what part of yourself
to another you have just brought

If you can live
each minute differently
doing only what you want
and never thinking of me

Then I hope you can change
and look to the past
and keep repeating
what makes our relationship last

Take away the hurt
and don't bring more sorrow
so in your arms
you can find me tomorrow

If you can honestly say
that you really don't care
then it will never matter
if I'm here or if I'm there

Who are you
my music man
blow in and out of my life
then reappear again

Distant phone calls
months between a touch
just when I lost hope
a presence I desire so much

Please stop the game
let me know if you're real
or just my imagination
wanting to feel

Love, hate
games and desire
why can't I be enough
to satisfy your fire

One day I'll sit down
and write you a letter
in it I'll tell you
it can only get better

I'll try to turn that lie
into the truth again
then maybe we could start over
and you could be my friend

I miss all those nights
of holding you near
when you made me smile
and wiped away my fear

Anything you wanted
I would do for you
except let you see
my true feelings show through

I was afraid to ask
if it was only me
for then I'd have to grow up
and face reality

I never got tired
of seeing your face
but I always felt
I was in someone else's place

Please just once more
let me hold your hand
and answer my question
on where I stand

No longer do I wish
for a touch upon my face
I'd rather be alone
than in someone else's place

I was told the only thing lacking in a
relationship is what you're not giving.
Sometimes the only thing lacking is reciprocity.

I'm tired of this feeling
but it just won't go away
Why won't you make up your mind
whether to leave or stay

Love just isn't enough
or so at least it seems
to always keep us together
and happily live out our dreams

But just what is missing
I guess I'll never know
for before you'll tell me
you'd rather just go

I love you, like I said
but that's not enough
for you to stay with me
like you said, that's just tuff

Right now what is happening
I'm too damn tired to figure out
I'm not sure I want to know anymore
what your love is all about

My Special Love

I have something special
it's a true and faithful love
so pure and understanding
it was sent from up above

So pure that I could never
look upon another face
and even consider
putting it in your place

Too understanding
for my own good
I forgive things
that no others would

This isn't love
it's just a trap
I can struggle within
but can't fight back

You put me here
four years ago
now you left but won't release me
because you don't know

Can anything from above
ever come to die
I know the answer
for this is why I cry

So I'll remain in your trap
and live in your hell
but will you ever release me
only time will tell

There's been something
that I've been meaning to say
but the words never come out
so I'll have to say it in my own way

I could always write
the words I couldn't speak
because when I'm with you
my heart makes me weak

I think you're special
so I need to know
if you really care
or if you could easily let go

You see, I'm not like that
I need someone near
someone to hold me close
and take away my fear

I can't be shared
with someone else
I have to be the one
or I'll be by myself

I am very special
in my own little way
and I need to find someone
to be with today

Someone who will
always be around
and ready to pick
me up off the ground

I want it to be you
who stays with me
if this is not what you want
then please just let me be

It's not the act that hurts it's the intention.

When you look at my face
what do you see?
Someone special
or just the same old me

Whey you gaze into my eyes
can it make you smile?
Or do you feel
that it's not worthwhile

When you hold my hand
is it for the touch?
Or just because
I want you to so much

When you awaken beside me
does it feel good?
Or just the same
as any morning would

When you hold me close
do you feel our love?
Or would you rather
give me a shove

This isn't a test
nor is it a game
I just want to know
if you feel the same

All of these things
are special to me
and I want to keep them
for all eternity

Sometimes it's love
sometimes it's hate
I don't want to be alone
but I'm going to have to wait

I want to be loved
and needed around
whenever I get lost
I want to be found

Fantasies mixed with freedom
never seem to come true
maybe that's why
I can't be alone with you

Am I not good enough
to share in your dream
be a part of your world
and play on your team

I'm at a time in my life
when I want to settle down
but when I look at you
I'm not sure what I've found

Love is never wasted, only the
lessons we refuse to learn.

Under the pitch black darkness
of a starlight sky
I sit alone
and wonder why

Why is no one holding me
or by the fire inside
why have I continued
to only run and hide

I want so much to feel
arms welcome me home
a soft kiss and an embrace
someone to call my own

I was always the one
who had someone to share
my life, my hopes, my dreams
someone who was always there

What did I do
to close every door
no more companions
no one to adore

Have I lost my appeal
does it matter anymore
did I let opportunity slip
through a secluded little door

Was there ever true love
that promised all
or just knocks on my door
until someone better came to call

I used to think I possessed
something special to share
my life, my love, my gifts
is there no one waiting there

Only loneliness and lost dreams
fill my day and night
I'm scared to think
I was just a fleeting sight

A companion to fill
the gap in someone's dream
someone to fill the space
until they found what they seem

From Ecstasy to Emptiness

From ecstasy to emptiness
writing through my pain
trying to get ahead
my path I can't explain

Why does it hurt
what takes so long
to work through the process
when will I belong

My heart feels open
but it's closed I'm told
I want to find someone
before I grow too old

Impatience persists
though I'm told to wait
I'm tired of feeling
no more to contemplate

Even if we find ourselves in a story we didn't start we have the power to write the ending.

What Lies Beneath

What lies beneath
your well-crafted words
perfected over time
so often heard

Messages transmitted
time and again
why you don't love
can we just be friends

Well worn lines
stolen from the pages
of books you study
a message for the ages

Too easily written
so quick to say
please leave me alone
you'll be better someday

Can't your heart feel
beyond a fleeting kiss
do you ever lie alone at night
and wonder what you miss

Life is filled with pressure
love is ripe with pain
until you can experience
you'll keep perpetuating a game

What do you desire
beyond your fear
a series of encounters
or someone to hold near

A trail of broken hearts
are left in your wake
you say you don't want that
but continue to only take

My experience was real
I opened my heart
only to find you gone
before we could start

A life of empty moments
filled with betrayal and pain
a path scattered with feelings
now walked in vain

I sit alone
by a creek gently flowing
reminded of a longing
of loneliness not knowing

How I created
this reality of doubt
When will someone come
and teach me what love's about

So quick to dismiss
a helping hand
Longing for a love
what drives my life's command

I created this solitude
but long for a connection
A fear of betrayals
leads to loss of affection

I dance alone
and drink my wine
as I long for a touch
what I created is mine

I long to hold
a hand to care
but quickly dismiss
who comes to share

White caps over rocks
an endless ebb and flow
I long to capture
what love wants me to know

*Time only heals the distance
between the heartbreak
and the present.
Love only heals what
you're willing to let go.*

Don't ask why
to someone close
for that's the person
who hurts you most

Don't ask questions
especially about love
for there's no right answer
that will come from above

Don't ask yourself
as you lie awake in bed
what you did wrong
or what you should have said

Questions are for losers
why is just a word
love is only for fools
who just like to be heard

Don't wonder why
they say I don't know
just like everyone else
they have no feelings to show

Trust and honesty
are just games we play
for in the end we only hear
I'm sorry but what can I say

Don't ask why
but be the first to laugh
for if you're not
it takes longer to pass

So live your life
for no one else but you
just don't ask me
what I plan to do

Chapter 9

Out of Control

He flew so high
he touched the sky
he had nothing to gain
but a lifetime of pain

He'd just lost it all
so he took a bad fall
he laughed, he cried
he almost died

But he was wrong
to sing a sad song
he didn't lose that much
someone had just numbed his touch

At first he couldn't see
how much he meant to me
he was given another chance to touch
someone he loved as much

Now he lives again
he's a lover and a friend
he'll never again have to hide
from a pain that's deep inside

Talk to me
I'll translate your pain
You have nothing to lose
but insight to gain

I can go deeper
than what you can
I can help you
become a stronger man

Let me uncover
your deepest fears
beyond your feelings
underneath your tears

Let me help you uncover
what you're afraid to face
then you can live
not in fear but in grace

Underneath your searching
lies passion untapped
what you long to feel
in your heart so tightly wrapped

Passion longs
to be unleashed
let me help you describe
the feelings you've kept beneath

Your intimate desires
your deepest fears
are safe with me
your heart I hold near

I know you don't love me
and that's ok
I want to help you
feel your heart today

If I can free
your locked up pain
you can begin to live
no longer in vain

I can translate
your feelings inside
that you can't tap
no longer will you need to hide

Let me free you
of your fears
I love you enough
to wipe away your tears

No tomorrows need you promise
unto me you will not live
I only want you to begin
not to take, but to give

Sweet memories await you
in your future so bright
no more darkness
I can give you the light

Please Take Care

I can't tell you
what to do
with your life

Even though
I wish I could

I don't know
how to say it
any other way

So please take care

Watch out for yourself
in everything you do

Please don't go so far overboard
trying to forget your problems
that you can never face reality again

Love hurts
Life hurts

Don't ask why
that's just the way it is

Too many people
ask that question

But nobody ever finds
the answer

Maybe that's because
there is no answer to find

Just remember nobody else in this world
is more important than you
and nobody ever will be

Maybe that's the answer
you have to
like yourself enough
to start with

But who does? . . .

So please take care

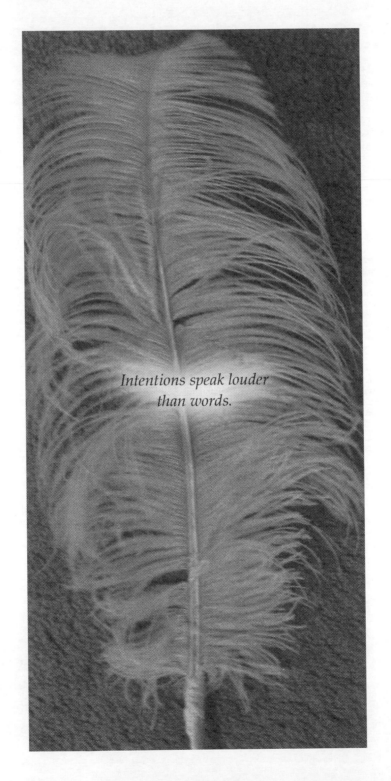

Intentions speak louder
than words.

Chapter 10

Lost

The days are getting better
but the nights are still the same
they remain lonely
filled with sorrow and pain

It is much easier
to hide in the sun
for then they can't tell
that I'm the lonely one

But the nighttime can't hide
my deepest of fears
as I sit all alone
surrounded by tears

My eyes are now blind
as I can no longer fight
I can't seem to tell
the dark from the light

You can either fall victim to it or rise above it.

I Wonder Why

I sit in the dark
and wonder why
and then I smile
and start to cry

As dawn creeps through
my window pane
I cry because
it's still the same

The day drags on
as I fill demands
all I want
is the touch of a hand

Sometimes I dream
about a smile
and then my day
seems all worthwhile

But then I sit
and wonder why
and then I smile
and then I cry

All I wanted
was a loving arm
someone to come
and protect me from harm

A friend to care
that wouldn't have to leave
someone to encourage me
and make me believe

But then I sit
and wonder why
and then I smile
and then I cry

I used to be able
to make people smile
I was happy and in love
for just a little while

I used to want
to make people happy
but it hurt too much
so now it's just me

I used to think I had
the only perfect love
but it was all a lie
that now lives far from above

I used to care
about what the future had in store
but my feelings have gone
it doesn't matter anymore

I can still love
but not in my old special ways
you took that away from me
on those sad and lonely days

I used to think I had
so much of myself to give
but now I have given too much
I'm just trying to live

I'm Not Crazy

I run to my room
and cry myself to sleep
trying to forget a pain
unexplainably deep

I sometimes feel so scared
but I don't know what of
sometimes I think it's pain
sometimes maybe it's love

Some people get me mad
when they always hold be back
they won't let me grow up
and make me live in a trap

So you see
it's not my fault I'm upset
it's just from all
the resistance I always get

Just because I cry
doesn't mean I'm insane
It only means I'm trying
to get rid of all my pain

Emotions are meant to flow freely . . . let them.

Lonely Is the Word

Lonely is when
you lie awake in bed
trying to recall
what you had said

Where it went wrong
when the hate began
why you can't love me
when you become a man

Going nowhere
without someone waiting
the pain from love
and bitter hating

Filling your days
with worthless tasks
you'll do anything
to not take off the mask

The feeling when it comes
you fight till it goes away
and wonder how much longer
you'll have to feel this way

You don't want to be told
you're something you've already heard
you never want to love again
lonely is the word

The little girl
you knew so well
is all grown up
and lives in hell

She can stay up late
to wait for you to come home
and cries herself to sleep
with her head on the phone

She can go out at night
and walk by herself
waiting for you to come
and take her off your shelf

She gets to fight her own fights
and suffer alone
on long lonely nights
she can call her own

Her childhood is gone
as she drinks from a cup
and waits patiently
for you to grow up

Lose yourself in daydreams,
not in people.

I've given so much
now it's my turn to take
I only feel anger
at night as I lay awake

Why me, I ask myself
all alone at night
everyday my feelings
I seem to have to fight

I only miss a dream
I dreamt so long ago
that will never come true
or help me to grow

But it's my new dreams
that I must push aside
because I'm afraid
that tomorrow they too, will die

Tired of being tired
scared of being scared
what lies waiting
is better left undeclared

Too afraid to ask
what you want with me
is there someone else
who you want to see

I have to know
but I'm scared to ask
this is the hardest
part of the task

The journey to love
or a life lived alone
too much sorrow
this is the life I've known

Created not out of jealousy
rather insecurity and doubt
I can never move on
until I know what it's about

Listen to what's not being said.

The Final Conflict

My feelings have gone
with the love you took away
no emotions are left
only yesterday

Remnants of our love
once cherished dearly
have now lost their meaning
for you're no longer near me

A part of my life
has now turned to dust
the wind blew it away
with one violent gust

In the past forever
it must now remain
never again will love
destroy my great domain

So no more pain
no more sorrow
will I let fill
my day tomorrow

But tomorrow never comes
so I'll just stop writing
for maybe if I give this up
I can stop the fighting

So you can hate me if you want
you can laugh at me, too
but I just can't let go
or ever stop loving you

If you want to leave
just turn and walk away
but you'll be in my thoughts
each and every day

I think this is what you want
you can't stand me anymore
I don't want apologies
or to be felt sorry for

I can't stand not holding you
or kissing your face
but now for me to do that
I'd be way out of place

This is hurting me bad
be my friend and help me through
try to make it easier for me
to forget about you

I'm sorry, I know
it was unfair of me to ask
but I just can't let go
at least not now, of my past

We can talk, we can cry,
we can laugh, we can scream
but will it ever let us
share another dream

I want to so bad
I need to so much
all I want right now
is to just feel your touch

Letting Go

Now I understand
why I can't let go
focusing on good-bye
afraid to say hello

Too much time alone
absorbed in reflection
too many tears
over every rejection

Too little adventure
diversions from myself
I need to focus
on abundance and wealth

I used to rebound quickly
surrounded by fun
where did I get lost
in a world of only one

Self-sufficiency is
the mask I wear
inside my lonely world
behind walls of despair

Forgetting my way out
losing the key
remembering there's a world
waiting just for me

I'm only missing me
not some other face
I created to comfort
me in this race

Trying to write
crying to express
caught in a trap
of misguided loneliness

Typing my tears
entertaining one thought
forgetting a way out
is the trap in which I'm caught

The Truth Behind The Smile

I awake each day
with a smile upon my face
wondering whose world
I could make a brighter place

Going to bed
I'd softly sigh
I'd made someone smile
but they'd made me cry

So life went on
and I'd awaken again
wondering who
I could make my friend

Then I went to bed
and I'd silently cry
knowing the truth
then my friendship I'd dry

This went on
for so many years
saying good-bye
with my nighttime tears

Then I wouldn't awaken
with a smile on my face
only tired eyes and lines
would show up in its place

As I now look back
and remember the smiles
I begin to wonder
if they were all worthwhile

You see, my friend
I got caught in a trap
one that wouldn't let go
and give myself back

I hope you'll see
over the years
that for every smile
you'll shed some tears

Reflections

Look upon
the gift and the taken
for what reasons
and might they be forsaken

Cherish them deeply
and to not another give
this is the special strength
in which love must live

Know of their difference
and each sacrifice
think to the future
before you move twice

Repay the debts
for a favor cast
of yourself give
and your love shall last

There is no room here
for selfish acts
they will leave you standing
too painful to look back

Now glance back
at your mistakes so many
were they worth it in the end
to be left without any

For it is for fools
this little love game
you must, to win it
both play the same

For in the end
to make it last
the stairway to heaven
brings back our past

Of this think hard
if of mistakes you can repent
but only if it's more
than just another lifetime spent

*Your voice, your desire, your story
fans the flames of creativity.*

Chapter 11

Rejection

You swept me off my feet
and laid next to me in bed
You promised me a future
but left me alone instead

From one lie to another
you travel quickly in time
I want you to understand
the rhythm of your rhyme

The longing for acceptance
the words I left unsaid
on that starlit night
you sent me alone to bed

I never saw it coming
the connection and betrayal
your lies I believed
another love I've failed

Starlight, starbright
I gaze alone at the sky
wondering who
wondering why

Just another confirmation
in a long line of rejection
as I continue to believe
I'll never find a connection

Someone who shares
my ideals and dreams
someone to hold me close
who can understand my screams

Loneliness and doubt
my companions on this road
waiting for an exit sign
is my wish too bold?

But it Wasn't Her

I was always there
when you needed
someone to lean on

But when I was there
you needed her

When you needed
someone to care for you
I tried to help you

But I was there
when you needed her

You needed
someone to show you the way
but I couldn't do it

Because I wasn't her

Now I realize
why you hate me
I was always there

But you wanted her

I only always
hurt you more
by trying to make up
for her not being there

Because you wanted her
but I was there

I'm sorry I
caused you so much pain
but I thought I could help you
But how could I

Because I wasn't her

A dream begins with a ripple of imagination.

Silently I cry
there aren't any tears
how can you express
the loss of so many years

The feeling is mutual
but not quite the same
the reason you don't cry
is because you gave me the blame

My feelings are mixed
my feelings are deep
I can never forget them
my feelings I must keep

I won't let you see
the way I feel inside
I might have lost a lot
but I'll always have my pride

What has happened
is now in the past
tomorrow I'll only remember the good
the memories of bad won't last

But the hurt will always be there
the scars will never heal
the pain of a love long lost
and my love not wanting to feel

So each time you look at me now
if you look behind my mask
you'll see the memories I carry
and the pain I feel from the past

That Wasn't Me

That wasn't me
who cried last night
too afraid to sleep
and shut off the light

That wasn't me
standing all by myself
waiting for someone
to take me off my shelf

That wasn't me
screaming out the door
at a long lost dream
that doesn't matter anymore

I'm more special than that
at least I used to be
but that was before
you took myself away from me

All those nights of rejection
and words that criticize
left lines on my face
and tears in my eyes

All I had left
was to fight for attention
and push aside a pain
too deep to mention

That's when this person
emerged from the night
who is hopelessly alone
when you turned out the light

You are the only one who can
block your progress.

The Little Boy

Whatever happened to that little boy
who tried to be a man
he used to make me laugh
and loved me for who I am

He used to cry and sing to me
no matter the time of day
he used to love and laugh with me
and he'd always find my way

But now the man has left
and just the boy remains
but all the little games he plays
causes me such pains

For the boy doesn't think twice
about anything he does
but then he wonders why
nothing is like it was

Why can't the boy give way
and be a man again
then we could be more than lovers
we could be good friends

The Legend Lives On

The legend lives on
like so may others
the memories of two
who used t be lovers

Our legend is special
and different from the rest
I was in love
but couldn't be best

We've both had our share
of broken hearts and pain
now you're leaving
why you can't explain

The legend is mighty
the legend is strong
to tell of it all
would take too long

For one cannot tell
of their whole life
there are too many joys
there's been too much strife

Our legend will be remembered
as a powerful love
that conquered all
but died up above

Some legends have morals
ours has none
it just says
there's never only one

Let our legend live
forever in your heart
then you won't feel lonely
and we'll never be apart

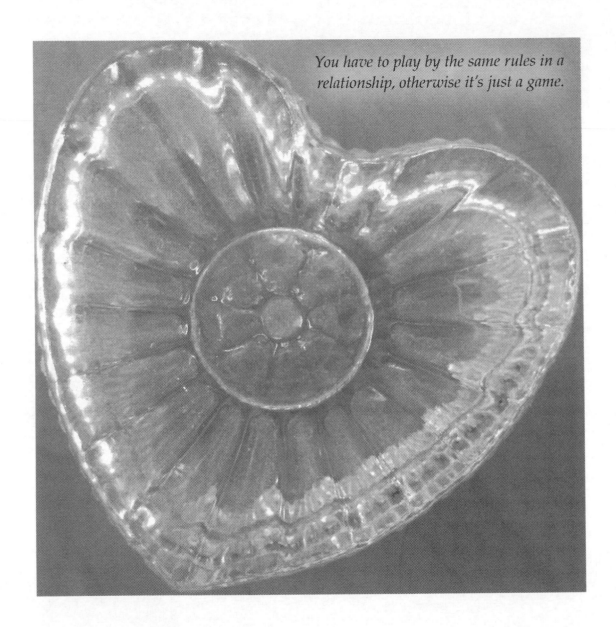

You have to play by the same rules in a relationship, otherwise it's just a game.

Chapter 12

Breakups

Remember in Silence

Remember me in silence
for words could never express
all the things we've gone through
and times I thought were best

Remember in the shadows
of your darkest nights
the joy that filled our hearts
and love's shining light

Remember the happiness
remember the joy
the games of your childhood
when you were still a boy

Remember the lessons
from mistakes you have made
forget of their pain
so to rest they may be laid

Remember in silence
of a love we once had shared
remember it for today
for tomorrow it won't be there

He's a brother
a friend
a teacher
He's always there

Whenever you
need him

To talk to
to cry to
to listen to
to laugh with

He's reality
love
sorrow
happiness

He's special
He's everything

He's gone

A Time to Forget

You just killed
the one who loved you most
so raise your glass high
and say good-bye with a toast

You just threw away
everything you said you were after
now you can fill your days
with thoughts of me and laughter

So don't feel sorry
and say you don't care
but you'll always feel something
deep inside somewhere

Remember not to think
about the love we did share
remember to always stand tall
remember not to care

So just laugh a lot
and don't cry at all
just don't think about someday
when again you will fall

But not because of me
I never left a trace
no scars were left on your heart
no lines added to your face

So now for you
there's only happy days ahead
don't forget to think about them
as you lie awake in bed

Now you have what you want
you're out on your own
but things can get lonely
with just yourself all alone

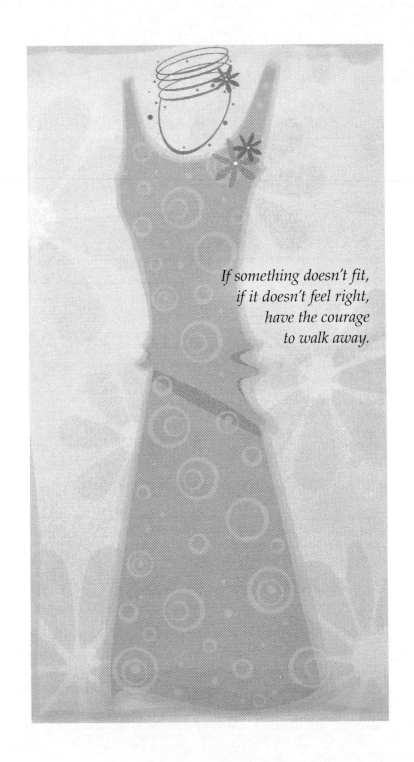

If something doesn't fit,
if it doesn't feel right,
have the courage
to walk away.

Moment By Moment

Moment by moment
our love slipped away
you said it was gone
lost to yesterday

Moment by moment
I stopped my pain
but the only way for me
was to make another gain

The moment felt right
I needed someone near
someone who could care
and take away my fear

The moment felt right
so I pushed the world aside
I was so vulnerable
with my arms open wide

The moment has changed
but I still feel the same
I can only hope
it's not just another game

The moment has changed
every moment with you
how can you still love me
after what we've been through

I must have been stupid
to ever have cared
I was pretty dumb
to have always been there

I must have been blind
to never see
how much you hated,
hurt and used me

You taught me a lot
especially about love
nothing is forever
or pure from above

I leave you now
without a tear in my eye
never again for you
will I let myself cry

Just this one last time
a tear from my eyes I'll shed
now only my heart will cry
as I lie awake in bed

I won't let my heart
rule over my head again
from a love that has grown
just out of a friend

My Friend, My Lover

I loved you once
you used to be my friend
but it seems to be gone now
it's ended again

So much has happened
these past three years
there wasn't enough laughter
to cover up the tears

We'll both always care
and we'll probably cry
but slowly it will pass
from the pain we won't die

It was never good enough
at least not for one
everyone said it was perfect
well, at least just some

I know I must leave you
but I want to hold you close
I hope you'll remember
you're the one I wanted most

Maybe in the future
our paths will cross again
and we can start over
and you can be my friend

If we were perfect we wouldn't still be around to learn lessons.

I cried for you today
like so many times before
but this time it hurt the most
for I miss you even more

I miss that happy, carefree smile
that used to light my world
It hurts because my dream of you
has now come all unfurled

I wanted you then
I needed you so bad
I honestly thought that you
were the only future I had

Thanks for showing me happiness
the kind we never could share
for we were too busy with ourselves
to realize the love that was there

You've been the greatest teacher
though you didn't even know
what I was learning
or that you taught me how to grow

But no one will ever know
of my true feelings inside
because these poems are the walls
in which I created to hide

For no one can truly understand
the way I feel for you
the feeling has changed, but it's still the same
it's gone but it's never through

I want him back
I love him so
the best thing I could do
was to let him go

I hurts so much
I feel so alone
finally I can see
how much I have grown

The pain shall leave
the pain shall stay
It's gone tomorrow
it's here today

Confusion and knowing
what you're doing is right
wondering why
as you lie awake at night

Loving, hating
needing, wanting
everyday my mind
they're haunting

Tomorrow brings the sunshine
another day alone
none of this would have happened
if I could just have left my home

Sometimes we hide behind our stories.
Sometimes our stories shed light on our reality.

This One's For You

You create your own guilt
no one gave that to you
people give you pain
there's nothing you can do

You can't help falling in love
even if you know it's a mistake
you have to prove them wrong
but losing yourself is the risk you take

He gave myself to him
he took me away from me
he promised me everything
then he set himself free

He kept everything he took
nothing can be replaced
but what he took won't help him
to him it's just waste

You hurt me so bad
you'll never know
I'll never again feel
a love inside me grow

You took away my touch
I can never feel again
you never gave me back my sight
you kept me blind until the end

All that's left now
isn't worth thinking about
disgust, hatred, lies
bitterness and doubt

But nothing is forever
you'll just die trying
but you know I don't believe that
so I'll just go on lying

The Best of Friends

Our love was wild,
pure and free
but it was too young and innocent
like you and me

You showed me love,
pain and joy
I let you live out
your life as a boy

You wouldn't grow up
within my arms
so you let go
with a flurry of storms

We don't have to remember
or win back our past
those feelings were yesterday's
and not meant to last

Good-bye forever
as my broken heart mends
the love has died
into the best of friends

From wedding bells
to friendship rings
is a painful change
to some it seems

But love, my child
is very strange
your life it forever
will rearrange

So don't let it hurt
for I can feel no pain
I've stopped the love
how I can't explain

I guess there's one love
you can't hide on a shelf
it's the love one feels
for their self

So friends we'll remain
for the rest of our lives
never again about marriage
will you have to think twice

You can never hurt me
I've felt deeper pain before
long before I let you
set foot inside my door

No man can ever conquer
my protected little world
the fortress is too strong
my dreams long ago unfurled

I won't allow it to happen
my heart will never break
I want no more to give
I just want to take

Yesterday's Love

Yesterday's love
is tomorrow's memories
filled with sadness
and hatred of me

Yesterday's love
was just a game
where rules were broken
but we lost just the same

Yesterday's love
will never return
in Heaven it will flourish
in Hell it will burn

Yesterday's love
was good and was bad
but it was only built on dreams
that I once had

Yesterday's love
was filled with fights
but we kept holding on
despite sleepless nights

Yesterday's love
was one of guilt and sorrow
it might anew
and come back tomorrow

Yesterday's love
was started by spite
we both knew the truth
but wouldn't face the light

Yesterday's love
might just be friendship
or maybe the love we had
we just let slip

Yesterday's love
thrived on desire
it tore apart dreams
and set goals on fire

Yesterday's love
we just couldn't take
we were both hurt too bad
by a little mistake

Yesterday's love
was sometimes good, I know
that's why I don't want
to ever let it go

Yesterday's love
has now ceased to be
you can forget it if you want
but it will always be remembered by me

But it hasn't stopped, damn it
it just hurts too much
not seeing your smile
not feeling your touch

This damn empty feeling
just won't go away
inside it keeps growing
it gets bigger each day

I need you with me
to hold my hand
I'm scared to be alone
by myself I can't stand

A love never dies
nor will my love for you
no matter what people say
I can't help but be true

The Dream

I dreamed of a boy
different from the rest
he could care and said so
that's what made my boy best

I dreamed of others
who could care and did, too
it hurt me to see them
I only believed in you

I dreamed a few years
and a lifetime of happiness
but when the fighting started
the dream just left

Then I dreamed
a sad thought of my past
deep down inside
I saw it couldn't last

This new dream I have
I want so much
I feel like dying
when I can't feel your touch

Please don't let my dream
ever go away
because now I know
I loved you more yesterday

Tears heal

It's Too Late To Rearrange

I wanted to kiss you
but is was strange
it's too late now
to rearrange

My life, I mean
everything was planned
it's too late now
to let it get out of hand

All of the bitterness
has now come out
all that's left now
is to scream and shout

I'm not the way I was
and you've changed too much
for us to feel the love
in one little touch

But why now
why not before
it's too late now for me
to open another door

I'm on a one-way street
and now the traffic has turned
another obstacle to overcome
something else from you I learned

But you know that's wrong
I've taught me
you knew all along
that I was too blind to see

I can't turn back
or take another road
this whole damn thing
is now too old

Too old to live
too young to survive
just like us
we can't stay alive

Like me right now
I don't know why
I can't say what I mean anymore
so I'll say goodbye

Thank You For Being a Friend

You've showed me pain
so deep I wept
I gave you so much
my soul you kept

You've showed me hate
and so much spite
I stay awake
and wonder each night

You've made me jealous
so much I can't trust
for everyone is after
revenge or lust

You've showed me a family
and for a while I belonged
but now things have changed
so we have a new song

You've showed me a love
and let me feel it grow
you taught me how to fight
and how to let go

You've showed me life
I no longer need to pretend
what else can I say . . .
Thank you for being a friend

Keep the lessons. Lose the blame.

Remember When . . . We Were Close

Quite a while
has passed me by
since I've come
to you and cried

but that same time
is equal to
the time I heard
my name from you

You always kept
on telling me
that I should live
my life for me

Remember how
you used to say
let the others
go their way

Then I'd get
so mad at you
and pray to God
it wouldn't be true

Well now I've done
what you have preached
and all my dreams
seemed so in reach

And ever since then
I have realized
that after I talk to you
tears fill my eyes

For everything you say
seems to come true
but I can't bear
this thought of losing you

So please promise me
your memories of me will never die
please tell me that
even if you have to lie

Now I've said
what I wanted to say
please don't forget
to think of me today

Fly By Night

Fly by night
in the blink of an eye
what once brought a smile
now makes me cry

A transition in time
a bridge to something new
not yet done with the past
without a future in view

What changed your mind
and lit the spark
was there ever a flame
or a dislike of the dark

A diversion carried away
or filling a lonely space
what do you see
when you gaze upon my face

Into the night
a moment flies by
to catch or let go
a dream come true or a lie

Fly by night
where are you going
what do you want
I can't stand not knowing

In a flurry you left
me alone at night
a dream slowly dies
in each morning's light

Fly by night
away from me
please let me know
what only your heart can see

Fly tonight
on the wings of your charms
from sunset to rise
hold me in your arms

People come
and stay for a while,
then they leave
without a smile

But when they're special
it hurts even more
especially when they leave
without closing the door

Just thank God
they stayed for a while
and thank them for letting you
make them smile

Remember the good times
forget the pain
keep the memories
so alive your heart can remain

For all life is
is a learning game
there are no rules
so nothing is the same

There is no right
there is no wrong
wherever you're put
is where you must belong

For again tomorrow
will shine the sun
you just gotta keep looking out
for number one

Goodbye my love
thanks for your time
too bad you can't stay
and always be mine

You've let another
take my place
just as you let me
somewhere else in space

Now there's someone special
that's in your life for you
I'm glad that you are happy
but what else can I do

Now she's the one
who lets you forget about me
she's the only one to ease your pain
so now love her for eternity

Goodbye my love
forever more
for in the end
I've shut my door

You've already let her
take your love from me away
we will never have tomorrow
but I'll cherish yesterday

In The End

We've been through a lot
these past few years
remember the laughter
and all of the tears

All of the confusion
all of that pain
trying to get ahead
when there was nothing to gain

We were lost in the confusion
like so many others
we just couldn't decide
if we were friends or lovers

But we're past that now
and we know where we are
and with that knowledge
our love can go far

Now I know
that on your love I can depend
remember only you
can make me smile in the end

Chapter 13

Insights

When dreamers grow up
the angels cry
a soul has lost it's sight
in the blink of an eye

No more wonder enlightens
the innocence of a child
reality is ripped away
by a flurry so wild

Growing up hurts
the initiation of pain
as the lessons are learned
of betrayal and vain

Why must it hurt
growing up, I mean
a child's innocence
is more loving and serene

The rights of passage
will they never end
puberty is the beginning
death is the end

In the pitch black of night
the stars light the skies
the illusion of heaven
twinkles in our eyes

A glimmer of hope
or a cruel masquerade
why wonder why
this is the life you've made

What are you thinking
deep inside your thoughts
your reality is only
the interpretation you bought

If you change your mind
can you really transform
the well worn path
of the life you've borne

The torturous reality
of an artist's mind
to the rest of the world
we're totally blind

Build on your imagination. Breathe
life into your dream every day.

I Am Love

I am love
who worships one
I am the seed
he is the sun

I thrive on the sun
but I, too, need the rain
for to get some happiness
you must give some pain

Love is the carrier
of this seed
the sun is who planted
this poisonous weed

The seed bears bitter sweetness
and the sun just makes it grow
the seed can't live by itself
which is all the sun needs to know

But the seed needs the sun
just to survive
love needs only one
to barely stay alive

I am love
powerful when not alone
only the sun can change
how much I have grown

I moved away
in search of happiness
only to find
that no such thing exists

I moved to love
in which I believed
only to find
it's taken but not received

I moved to hope
of a better tomorrow
only to find
it filled with sorrow

I moved away
from all my tears
only to find
more terrifying fears

I moved into a world
I thought was filled with care
only to find
I was the only one there

I moved to freedom
that I thought I knew well
only to find myself
in a different kind of hell

Maybe it's time
for me to move on
to see what's in store
in tomorrow's new dawn

For you are moving backward
and I, ahead
I need something more
than just a companion in bed

Confessions of a True Love

There is no such thing
as a true love
that lasts forever
with happiness from above

Nothing on this earth
is natural and pure
but people are about the worst
of that I am sure

You have loved before
I was not the first
so before you even met me
our true love bond had burst

How can a love be true
when it sometimes changes to hate
or when you think so fondly of
someone you used to date

But it's not your fault
nor is it mine
the most we can do
is share a little of our time

Life was not created
for us to analyze
Love was not made
to measure by its size

Truth cannot be doubted
or thought of as a lie
Trust is something you have to earn
until the day you die

Respect should only be given
of it you should never ask
Responsibility is only as hard
as you make every little task

Mistakes aren't the judge
of what a person is like
Mysteries just always happen
throughout the day and night

Fantasies are forever present
not easy for one to see
Forever is a place that's never reached
and will always remain empty

It's better to be alone than with the wrong person.
The wrong person lines a path with lies.

Desire

Little boys
shouldn't play with fire
for they only get burned
by misguided desire

Their innocence leaves
and confusion takes its place
then no longer can a smile
be seen upon their face

Then soon comes love
infatuation in disguise
and soon after that
tears and hatred fill their eyes

Revenge is next
followed by sorrow
there are no more games
to brighten up tomorrow

So watch where you look
with your imagination so wild
and try to remember
that you're still just a child

Don't play with fire
you're better off in the dark
for a fire is lit
by the smallest little spark

But Why I Don't Know

Friends are there
to share and care
but then they go
and life goes on

But why I don't know

Families will stay together
through thick and thin
and all kinds of weather
but then one day
each must go away

But why I don't know

Wars are won
and wars are lost
some with little meaning
and some with much cost
filled with blood and destruction
with many lives lost
and life goes on

But why I don't know

We make mistakes, big and small
we make mistakes one and all
but we never learn as we make them again
till the end of time it will never end
and life goes on

But why I don't know

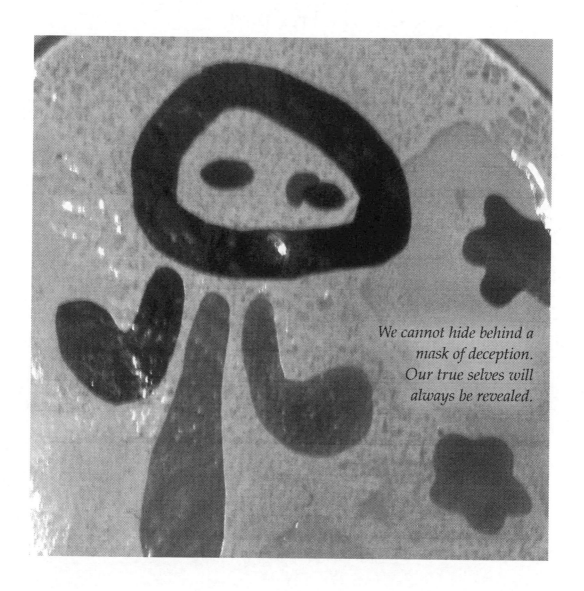

We cannot hide behind a
mask of deception.
Our true selves will
always be revealed.

The Free Bird

To you, I give the Free Bird
who seems to fly so free
he appears to fly in carefree freedom
the kind always wished for you and me

But look closely when you look at him
and I think you'll finally see
that the Free Bird doesn't really seem
in any one place to be free

You always see him flying
above the land or sea
he will never stop anyplace
and claim that place as free

You might be too young to see
but I think you'll understand
freedom is never taken or given away
by anyone else but man

So you'll have to wait
and soon Free Bird will come
to grant you what you want the most
he'll grant you your freedom

But you must always realize
that on that very same day
if Free Bird doesn't feel it's right
he'll take your freedom away

For what is freedom anyway
just doing whatever you please
remember the more you grow up
the more you'll have to face responsibilities

So is freedom then only for a child
whose life seems so pure and true
if you think that's so you're only taking
your freedom away from you

For everyone is as young as they want
and everyone has many responsibilities, too
but no one has ever been sure of their freedom
at least now there's one person, you

It's Lonely at the Top

I am a special person
I'm different from the rest
I have lived within life
that's why I'm the best

I've been able to help
so many people live
I can change things
myself I'm able to give

I am lucky I met you
for not many my age have known
what it's like to be loved
or to feel a love have grown

I am older than most
in many ways
older in experience
not in days

I might not be missed
by some when I'm gone
but from lessons they've learned from me
I shall live on

I miss them all, though
I miss them a lot
for you only live once
that's what I've been taught

I hope there will be another
who can give you as much as me
then you can always smile
and you might begin to see

For the world will keep on turning
for only me it will not stop
that's why it's always
so lonely at the top

The Impossible

Why do people
always only want
what they know
they can't get
and won't settle
for anything less

Why do we continue
to torture ourselves
day after day

Is that the only thing
that keeps us going

Working and hoping
for something that's
impossible to reach

Is that all
that life is

Just a cruel game
that keeps us
running in circles
trying to find
the impossible

Because we know
that if we were ever
to reach for something
within our grasp

We'll have what
we want
so there will be
no reason to
carry on anymore

The Trap

Life is nothing more
than a big trap
you enter it when you're born
there's no way out

No matter how hard
you fight
you only get in
deeper and deeper

Some people
go mad
trying to get out
of this horrible trap

Others just take shortcuts
trying to forget reality

Maybe they can't
stand it
maybe they just don't want to see it
can't face the truth
or want to forget it

Until finally
when it's all over and done with
we finally see
we understand
but it's too late now

All our lives we've tried
to fight the trap
now all our energy
is gone
there's no more strength
to fight back anymore

No more shortcuts that we can take

Finally we're able
to accept life
the way it is

But then it's too late

Because that's when
we die

Let the colors of your imagination run wild.

Chapter 14

Rise

Blood Sweat and Tears

Blood, sweat and tears
we've come to know them well
we've been through each and every one of them
in heaven and in hell

Everyday of our lives
we've lived within their walls
we even got so caught up in them
we couldn't hear each others calls

It took us so long
to get through the hell
whether or not we'll make it
only time will tell

Too many barriers
still stand in our way
can we overcome them
maybe someday

How we learn and how we love is up to us.

Living apart
but loving so much
remembering the smile
needing the touch

Lonely nights
and dreams of you
wishful thinking
that I pray will come true

Always too busy
there's never enough time
to be alone with you
forever mine

Selfish people
with narrow minds
never understanding
mine and your kind

Special moments
that will always be treasured
moments of a love
that will never be measured

Frustration and joy
combined with time
too many battles
before you'll be mine

Trust and jealousy
keeping us apart
each time love is destroyed
each time a new start

Ups and downs
circles and signs
we never know which
confuses our minds

This is the life
in which I must live
to keep you mine
myself I must give

I Really Need You

Another year
has come to pass
through heaven and hell
our love will last

True love and pride
forever will strive
all we need is each other
to stay alive

I wish I could show you
what you mean to me
but that would take forever
until eternity

Our love is good
pure and true
all my strength and happiness
comes from you

I love you
with all my heart and soul
our love will last forever
this I know

You have a place in me
deep inside
and you'll remain there
even after I've died

So love me gentle
pure and true
make it last, babe
because I really need you

Ashes to Ashes, Dust to Dust

God created life
we created love
both were a dream
created with hope from above

Each had good intentions
but destiny is never known
when surrounded by destruction
how could either one have grown

But God's will
must be stronger than ours
maybe He knew
He had a good cause

But if you look closely
life, too, is dying
it's a slow painful death
just like our lying

Ashes to ashes, dust to dust
everything will soon become
just another memory of the past
and then again we'll be one

For like the ashes we are
just memories of an old fire
the dust has settled and is a remnant of
everything that's been destroyed by desire

Surrounding the ashes and inside the dust
is something waiting to be recreated
a hopeless past lies wanting there
to live again – an eternity it has waited

Lessons are the stepping stones that line our path.
They build a bridge to our future.

The road that we have traveled
has been a hard and rocky one
but at the end of every rainbow
I promise you the sun

After all the battles
and wars were complete
we were left standing together
the others lay in defeat

For when love is present
it conquers all
even in the end
it helps us stand tall

but there's still a long journey
that lies ahead
to help us through
remember what I've said

I've talked about the rainbows
and the sun shining through
just remember whatever happens
I'll always be in love with you

I promise you the sunshine
I'll take away the rain
if we can walk the path together
I'll take away your pain

Keep moving forward. Sometimes we don't heal but adapt to a new reality.

Fly Away

I'm giving you the Free Bird
spread your wings and fly away
if you really love me
you'll return for me someday

But there's a whole world out there
that you've been waiting to see
and there's a lifetime of tasks to complete
before you'll come back for me

But you are the Free Bird
can't you see
no matter where you go
if you stay, you won't be free

I wish you luck
in your long journey away
I hope you find what you're after
and find your freedom someday

But be careful in your search
and don't forget where you left from
remember there's people waiting
and home's a place to come

Chapter 15

Starting Over

Chapter Two

The next part of my life
will be better, I can tell
for this time I won't live
in heaven or in hell

I'll find a peaceful place
somewhere in between
where there is no such thing as love
and people can't be mean

I'll live my life in privacy
forgetting about the past
for now the only thing I can be sure of
is nothing will ever last

No tears of joy or sorrow
no cuts will be left bleeding
in my heart I'll feel no pain
for now I've stopped the needing

I no longer wish
for a touch upon my face
I'd rather be alone
than in someone else's place

Encore

My act was so good
not even you could tell
that deep down inside
I was going through hell

During the day
I could smile and be bright
but the nights were lonely
filled with sorrow and fright

They believed me when I said
that it was best for me
but that is not true
I'll hurt for eternity

I want to begin
to play the part
of us in love
with a whole new start

I'm putting up my costume
I'm asking you to come back
but how will you know
if it's just another act

Faith is not blind, we are.
Let faith light your path.

Memories paint the scene
of a lifetime gone by
The foundation from which
you stumble or fly

Safety or courage
the choice is yours
Consequences are the result
you are the cause

Reflection is not
being in the past
Just a consideration
of what you want to last

Never pretend
that you don't know
You're only blocking
the opportunity to grow

Risk has rewards
setbacks and success
How you interpret
is up to you, I guess

Let go and live on
conquer your fears
Live your life
for many years

Thanks for Breaking My Heart

Thank you
for breaking my heart
opening me up to feelings
where the healing can start

Broken wide open
is the only way
for healing to happen
as I face each day

Diving deep into the pain
and feeling the fear
brings clarity of intention
to attract what I hold dear

Total acceptance
not judgment and lack
I want to love again
and get my life back

We are destined to repeat mistakes
until we learn our lesson.

Tomorrow Belongs To Me

Yesterday belongs
to broken dreams
and many lessons
that life's not what it seems

Yesterday belongs
to sleepless nights
and teary eyes
after too many fights

Yesterday left me angry
and very insecure
a little too grown up
and very demure

Today I struggle
to overcome my fright
of living alone
in the dark of night

Today I hold on
to a childhood lost
that I will bring back
at any cost

Today I must
begin new dreams
and forget yesterday
and those awful screams

Tomorrow will be
a happier life
free from struggle
free from strife

For as far as
my eyes can see
tomorrow belongs
to me

Memories are like pictures
left painted in our thoughts
they keep appearing in our eyes
like old photograph snapshots

They are special to no one
save only ourselves
until we fill another bottle up
and place it among the shelves

We share them sometimes
but only with a few
for some are too painful
like a love you once knew

But through the years
the bad memories fade away
soon only good thoughts
will paint themselves to stay

Everyone has a story someone in the world needs to hear.

The Good-bye Poem

I ran into you today
in between the lines
as I sat alone in my room
flipping pages in my mind

You suddenly appeared
behind each and every poem
through tears of joy and sadness
my thoughts began to roam

History repeats itself
despite lessons we learn
the path is always familiar
lighted by emotions which forever burn

I never see it coming
as I hide behind my rhymes
the rhythm of my life
is the same every time

Abscence makes
the heart grow colder
as memories divert
to a long lost shoulder

The touch loses feeling
alone in the night
fear becomes reality
in the cold morning light

Rainbows are for dreamers
whose imaginations run wild
and get lost in a world
created by a lonely child

Say good-bye to tomorrow
hello yesterday
back to the beginning
I'll find another way

About the Author

Tami Belt is a natural-born storyteller. From changing the ending of ghost stories as a child to writing poetry since the age of 12, stories have saved her life. She wanted to be a rock star when she grew up but couldn't sing on key so she sings the praises of others as founder of Blue Cube Marketing Solutions, a public relations company.

www.1bluecube.com
www.writesofpassage.co
www.1writesofpassage.wordpress.com

Printed in the United States
By Bookmasters